Debbie MacKinnon worked as Art Director at
Dorling Kindersley and Frances Lincoln. For the last 12 years
she has written, developed and created her own books
for young children. Among her many successful titles are
a range of exciting photographic books for pre-schoolers
with the photographer Anthea Sieveking, including the
Right Start series and the Surprise, Surprise! board books.

Anthea Sieveking trained in photography at the
Oxford School of Art and now specialises in pictures of
children and babies. Her many titles with Debbie MacKinnon
for Frances Lincoln include the Eye Spy series and
Baby's First Year.

Abby

Brian

Camilla

David

Henry

Isabel

Janine

Kevin

Lee

Max

Nick

Oliver

Polly

Quentin

Rosie

Sophie

Tom

Ursula

Victor

Wendy

Edward

Flora

Gary

a b c d e f g h i j k l m n o p q r s t u

My First
ABC

Debbie MacKinnon

Photographs by Anthea Sieveking

F

FRANCES LINCOLN
CHILDREN'S BOOKS

n o p q r s t u v w x y z a b c d e f g h i

Xanthe

Yasmin

Zack

Abby's apple

Brian's book

Mary had a little lamb
and other animal rhymes

with photographs by Anthea Sieveking

Camilla's car

David's doll

Edward's elephant

Flora's frog

Gary's guitar

Henry's house

Isabel's ice-cream

Janine's jack-in-the-box

Kevin's kangaroo

Lee's ladybird

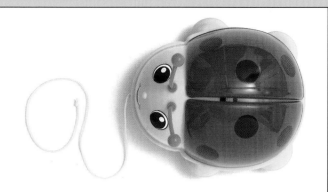

Max's mobile

Nick's numbers

Oliver's oranges

Polly's pool

Quentin's quilt

Rosie's rabbit

Sophie's sandpit

Tom's teddy

Ursula's
umbrella

Victor's vacuum cleaner

Wendy's wheelbarrow

Xanthe's xylophone

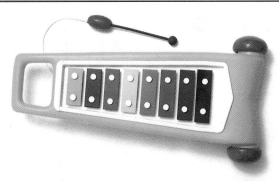

Yasmin's yacht

Zack's zebra

For my parents – D.M.

For Margaret – A.S.

First published in Great Britain in 1992 by
Frances Lincoln Children's Books, 4 Torriano Mews,
Torriano Avenue, London NW5 2RZ
www.franceslincoln.com

This paperback edition 2007

British Library Cataloguing in Publication Data available on request

ISBN 978-1-84507-742-6

Printed in China

1 3 5 7 9 8 6 4 2

MORE TITLES FROM
FRANCES LINCOLN CHILDREN'S BOOKS

BABY'S FIRST YEAR
Debbie MacKinnon
Photographs by Anthea Sieveking

"Happy Birthday, Jack! Welcome to the world."
From one day to one year old, charting first smile,
first tooth and first crawl, we celebrate all the
landmarks of a baby's first year.

ISBN 978-0-7112-2128-4

EYE SPY SHAPES
A Peephole Book
Debbie MacKinnon
Photographs by Anthea Sieveking

What shape is fun to play with? What shape flutters in the breeze?
Listen to the clue, look at the picture, peep through the peephole –
then turn the page to see the surprise!

ISBN 978-1-84507-711-2

AWAY IN A MANGER
Debbie MacKinnon

This simple retelling of the nativity, with inspiring photographs,
captures the true spirit of Christmas. The book includes
clear instructions on how to stage a nativity play, advice
and ideas about designing costumes, and the music and
words of the children's carol 'Away in a Manger'.

ISBN 978-1-84507-557-6

Frances Lincoln titles are available from all good bookshops.
You can also buy books and find out more about your favourite titles,
authors and illustrators on our website: www.franceslincoln.com